Numeralla Dreaming

poems by Mercedes Webb-Pullman

The following have been published previously:

Dangelong	Danse Macabre journal #45
First catch your trout	4th Floor journal 2009
Goodbye	Poets for the People, poetry from Lembas 2009
The day the camels came	Swamp journal #8 as 'Camel Time'

Numeralla Dreaming

#1

Title:	Numerella Dreaming
Author:	Mercedes Webb-Pullman
Publisher:	Bench Press
Address:	Doctor's Common, Mt Victoria, Wellington 6011
Format:	Paperback

Publication Date: January 2012

ISBN: 978-0-473-19860-2

Numeralla Dreaming

"Against the ruin of the world, there is only one defence — the *creative act.* ..."

Kenneth Rexroth

Numeralla Dreaming index

4th March	6
Blyton's sheep	7
Morphine clarity	8
Dangelong	10
Diptheria	11
Driven	12
Finding gold	13
First catch your trout	14
Funny how the garlic	16
Geoffrey's grandmother	17
Gnocchi	18
Goodbye	19
Bones	20
Grandfather's well	21
Hangman Gully after the fire	22
Set fires	23

Numeralla Dreaming

Logged out	24
Mount Numeralla	25
Night fishing	27
Night vision	28
Outside the fence	29
Planting Apple	30
Rabbits	31
Snakebite	32
Snakescript	35
Spring berries	36
Steve Primmer	37
The day the camels came	38
The fox	40
Tickling fish	41
Author bio	42

Numeralla Dreaming

4th March

today an eagle
soaring wings fixed above me
inscribed spirals in the air
over the valley
like a young child
home from school
who's just learned
the letter O

Blytons' sheep

they're bunched up on the river-flat
like wheel spokes
facing centre

in the hub
one trembling sheep
head trapped
in a white plastic
shopping bag
plunges and
pirouettes
its attempts
to get free

the rest
backed safely away
stare thoughtfully

Numeralla Dreaming

Morphine clarity

this blue gum glows; each part
from honey ant cascade
to budding leaves
star light
held in perfect tension
edges form and close together
this leaf will have this edge forever

not an apple tree
elevating over a meadow
in Breton-Finisterre
while Jacob wrestled
with his angel
and how Gauguin spent years
in tropical abundance
yet his most convincing flowers
were dream-Japanese, still burning
from the hands of the mad Dutchman

Paul grew sun-flowers in Tahiti
they were never the same

shine grows
on blood-red node
where leaf begins
incandescent line
distorts the space
it moves within
pulses and beats
its soul-tapping dance -
does it move you
grasshopper
or do you move it?

streams weave
along the trunk
rivulets of dark lights
glistening on wet ink highways
ants jostle-carry manna
honey formed from rot
tap tap feelers meeting
hello, hello,
I'm going this way

Numeralla Dreaming

dark bark patches
form from negative space
groupings, patterns
intimately change
ripple-pulse
outside and in
this pattern of ants
up and down
this pattern of tree
moving life around

Numeralla Dreaming

Dangelong

It's a long way – you have to
really want to go.
Drive across Rock Flat,
turn first left
along the gravel road
that skirts the creek,
go through three gates, and park
where the old swing bridge
spans the gorge.
Walk across the sky.
Follow the creek down; there are trout
in pools there, older and smarter
than you. Watch for snakes in tussocks
see where land folds
in frozen waves of quartz -
the Kydra reef, gold and Chinese graves –
there's a clearing on a knoll
right in front of you
where wedge-tailed eagles
gather in groups
and walk around on the ground
like men who wonder
how it feels
to fly.

Numeralla Dreaming

Diptheria

On Stockyard Creek
spot-marked by simple crosses
five children died
in two nights
a hundred years ago

pioneer child,
she blazes in bed
like a secret,
shaved skull
a dome of baking heat,
eyes streaming pain
or closed, beaten
in delirium

nostrums of calomel
don't halt the slow
strangulation
as throat membranes
thicken, days grind by

until all heat is gone
her bones
sink deadweight
into the mattress

something recedes
at impossible speed

Jane, 11 years

Driven

How it started – you took skulls
painted them bright primary colours
some glitter, shards of mirror
ribbons like garlands around them -
they sold well to the ski crowd

then you gathered bones
and more, an ossuary
claimed eagle bond
half shuffle dance with chant and rattle
accessed the culture
with little black pills
non-stop for days
popping shakers in the truck
shaking and rattling
trying to stitch it all together
patch-working
into something better

until you hanged yourself one night
in the shed behind the house
while your wife tidied her kitchen.

It's 4 am. A truck
works its way up Loginhole hill
shifts gear, grinds harder.
Bones glow in the headlights
dance in and out of shadows -
dawn rattles at the morning

Numeralla Dreaming

Finding gold

Dismounted, leading horses
uphill through rocks
we followed gold
backwards from the river traces,
searching for surfaced veins
in baking heat, so dry
flies fought on my skin
to drink my salty sweat,
until in a small creek-side clearing
we halted, set up camp
and sat inside the smoke.
Low clicks from Peter's metal detector
blended with cicada shrill, background
leather creaks of horse gear
and the quiet shift of twigs burning,
acrid wallaby-tinged
dog bush over-riding
gum scented wood smoke
in the glassy heated air -
electronic beep pierced -
we dug, sieved soil, unearthed
some rusted metal blobs
identified as hob nails,
sole remainders of boots,
and a crude metal bullock hobble,
searched further, found
a square of barren pounded ground,
traces of bark walls, caught
in the process of melting back to earth
a careful hearth of river stone
covered in star-flowered creepers,
and a gold snake swift as flame.

Numeralla Dreaming

First catch your trout

pan-fried
in cast iron
over redgum fire
beside the river
where smoke and mist
      twist together

sautéed in butter
with almonds
and cream
a splash of white wine
liberal parsley

poached in wine
picked off the bone
and chilled,
floated through
colourful, seasoned aspic

rubbed with salt
finely chopped herbs
rosemary, thyme
oregano, sage
crushed garlic
and smoked all day
over quince wood

smoked, then pulled apart
packed in jars
with good olive oil

this requires some
preparation
have a large pot
of acidulated water
on a rolling boil
unhook your trout
and drop it in.

Numeralla Dreaming

death will be
instantaneous.
the fish
curls in a circle
head touching tail
and the flesh
when you eat
is pale
blue

did I mention
pan-fried
beside the river?

Numeralla Dreaming

Funny how the garlic

I braided a rope of garlic today.
The green hairs, autumn planted
have grown to these
purple globes
already paper-bagged.
After years of empty seasons
this is good.

I'd almost forgotten how,
had to do it backwards,
as once I braided my hair
making a heavy rope
that lay between my shoulder-blades,
snaking down my spine
so my breasts parted and pointed,
and you did that
slow thing with your tongue,
grazing from peaks to valley,
humming deep in your throat,
while my fingers
flickered in my hair
and sometimes
the braid was
abandoned.

Sometimes I coiled my hair
high on my head
fixed with a pair of chop-sticks.

Later, with me riding above you
you reached up,
took out the sticks
and laughed, as my hair
tumbled down over us
a curtain
for our cave.

Now I wear my hair short.
I hadn't thought of you in years.
Funny how the garlic
brought you back.

Geoffrey's grandmother

where birch thickets
cover banks in the river curve
Kings Creek emerges

fireplace
foundations
some chimney rock
by the fire-trail trace
bones of the cottage
where Geoffrey's grandmother
was born and raised
where women left alone
shot a stranger from fright
when he came to their door
out of the night

his people wrapped him
in bark like a parcel
after ceremony and singing
then left him
lying in the creek bank
just there
below where
the stockyard used to stand

Numeralla Dreaming

gnocchi

it took ages to find
the right potatoes here – floury
(back there I'd walk outside
and dig them up, best Blyton stock
they mashed like meringue, so light
or grew a golden crust beside the roast)

with a fork I prick each tuber twenty times
(raking slashed grasses, autumn dried
over the potato bed, layered with ash,
compost and soil, all level; when dark
green leaves appear, the hilling starts)

dry them, place in a hot oven to bake
until skins crisp, break open to steam
and while still hot, push through a grater

work in flour with ring-freed fingers
(this is the soothing part;
kneading dough, feeling change)
if it's sticky, add more flour

cut ball into portions, always cover
cut surfaces with flour drifts, roll
each portion into snakes
then take a fork, prongs down

make 1" cuts along the snake
(cover cuts with flour)
press each piece against the fork
with your thumb leaving lines
on one side, a dent on the other

place on a floured tray to dry
and freeze or use immediately

(the night Terry arrived
with prawns and oysters
I made a Frida Kahlo sauce
with gnocchi; how easy
when the wattle tree danced
outside my kitchen window)

Goodbye

goodbye smells musty, like old clothes
lost in the back of the wardrobe

dusty, like words on a scrap of newspaper
that flutters from an opened book

goodbye smells like an old man who smokes
and ate garlic last night, and the night before

warm, like tarmac in the centre of town
in summer, after a storm has passed

goodbye smells like coffee brewing
somewhere close, for someone else

like the kerosene taste in my throat
in the airport departure lounge

like your sweater, grabbed in error;
again you are here. my eyes break.

Bones

A kangaroo killed by the roadside
months ago
becomes earth;
the stench at first
a wall detoured around

then scraps of skin
stick dry and tatter
over bones, a cage,
a wrecked tent,
flesh melted away
into ant holes,
cracked clay, small rocks
in its bed

scattered bones
not obviously
kangaroo -
new grass
grows through

bone pieces, small
as teeth, indistinguishable
from quartz lumps
between clumps of grass
unless you focus closely - peer
into delicate, intricate shapes
like flowers – paws?

Numeralla Dreaming

Grandfather's Well

pulled up in a heavy
galvanised bucket
hand over hand
forty feet or more
through the dark throat,
this water holds light
splintered and twitching
in the bottom

strange place for a well
on top of a hill
but a dowser walked
a hundred years ago
found streams closest
to the surface here
where Geoffrey's grandfather
started digging

thoughtful water, spring fed
underground, a stream
that sneaks, drips
down runs of rock
collects in cracks to overflow
trickles
taking in darkness
and cold, even in
midsummer, icy
ghost of winter

Jean "We had to pull
twenty buckets between us
before school"

the filled containers
drip sweat, like you
and in one
bumbling its blind way
against the edge
again and again
a small white frog
with no eyes

but you are too busy
counting buckets of water
to see

Numeralla Dreaming

Hangman Gully after the fire

it swept up from the creek
annihilated ground cover
branches, leaves
shrubs, mosses
creepers, lichen from the rocks
even their ashes, sucked
into the maelstrom
no birds left, no animals —
a clean slate, sterilized
by the bomb impact
of fireball

only trunks remain
upright like fingers
pointing to something
in the sky
half black, half white
vertically striped
living flesh now charcoal
on the fire-hit side
like fused images
of a nuclear blast

the horses don't like it
shift uneasily
suck air for scents
twitch ears
nothing to smell, nothing to hear
but some glowing green blades
lacking branches
grow direct from tree trunks
here and there
like tiny banners of hope

Numeralla Dreaming

Set fires

Scarlet winked
from all the mountain flanks
and up against the horizon
crimson worms writhed and blinked.

If you'd been closer, near Sunshine, say
you'd have heard the numbing red roar
like a wave of rage that never ebbs;
with gunshot blasts trees explode,
branches crash and vaporise
in searing heat.

From here beside the Numeralla river
the burning-mountain-top horizon
psychedelic pyre showed
a selfish Armageddon.

The koala colony
died as it once survived;
quietly, without fuss
for the local
bush fire brigade
training exercise.

Logged out

Where have the trees gone?
Everything looks wrong,
skyline's changed, horizon
fallen, the world
closer than I thought

but this is the right track.
Where have the trees gone?
Along Good Good fire trail
snagged-up piles
like bones, ready to burn.

We follow logging tracks
to a ridge above the Badja;
where have the trees gone?
A vast wasteland valley -
scattered debris, tree trash.

Jackie spreads like a starfish
over a stump, once her favourite
midday shade tree, can't comprehend;
where have the trees gone?
Chris counts time ringing her.

In Kyoto an artist grinds his ink,
takes paper made from Chris's trees
meditates deeply, paints what he sees;
bare mountains -
where have the trees gone?

Numeralla Dreaming

Mount Numeralla

A youth, for initiation
is sent to the mountain
to find matchstick crystals
growing from quartz rocks
and there to choose
or be chosen by
his personal power, his *alcheringa;*
'you will know it, it will know you'.

He must live alone
find food and shelter where he can
without tools or weapons
apart from mind and hand
and speak not one word.

'Stay away' *kadaitcha* man
speaks in his *dreamtime* voice.
'I will find you when you've made
the right choice. I will know.'

Moon of fish, moon of fires
moon of meat and *corroboree*
have come and gone, and still
he searches. He has found
crystals, but none that speak.

Tonight, as the moon moves into snake
his tribe prepares to walk
down the cold mountains to the coast
for winter. Without his people
how can he stay here? Still no crystal
calls, though he listens harder.

He sees the fires -
how far away his family seems.
The path back to camp
blocked by *kadaitcha* man -

Numeralla Dreaming

step back, and the spectre disappears.
Death, if he returns
without fulfilling his quest.
Through night fully dark, he hears
movement on the path, and hides.
Death, if he speaks. He sees

enemy scouts
who may attack
for women, or for food.
No time to raise warning -
from the ground he grips a rock
and launches himself
naked, silent as sky
into the enemy. In camp,
kadaitcha man stiffens,
turns to the mountain.
A flash of light erupts
rainbow colours.
The tribe moves out.

Next year, *kadaitcha* man
walks directly to bones
in the mountain, finds
in the youth's hand, a crystal
and in the Dreamtime way
the youth becomes the mountain -
not dead, just sleeping
until he's needed again.

Night fishing

I light a twig fire
near where you fish

flames blow and twist
flick quiver-gold shifting
filigree veils over black
velvet shadows,
staccato splinters
of shade and light
hypnotic
as river acapella
as reeds breathing breeze;
everything dances
everything sings

even me, watching from the light
and you in the dark, fishing

Night vision

Darkness leant
against my windows.

On the shed roofline
a looming apparition
with mechanical
swivelling head;
basilisk headlights
blink
focus
intent

on me
reflected in the window
through his image -

me
and a sooty owl
in a black sky
shining.

Numeralla Dreaming

Outside the fence

Where the river bends
and thrusts against granite banks
I found axe heads
seed-grinding holes in rocks
and old charcoal, a shell midden
marking a summer plenty site
good place to sit
as water told its stories
and redgums bent to listen.

In midday heat when shimmer
moved the air around me
I saw shapes in the gully below the cemetery
that vanished as clouds masked the sun,
the river fell silent, air cold.
Later, researching gold, I read
of Chinese miners, their tunnel,
a tragic accident, hints of body
desecration for the treasure in their pigtails.

Bert talked about it once -
we were drinking rum, and he
hauled out some old memories
giving them a shake. His grandfather
as a young man, start of the first Depression
and his mates, jealous of Chinese miners
taking gold that should be theirs
blew up their tunnel.

'How many were in there?' I asked
'A couple of dozen, I suppose

one crawled back out, but he died.
Only the cook at the camp was left
and he didn't stay long.' The pause
that followed filled up
with questions.

Later he showed me outside the cemetery
where suicides and other non-believers lie.
His grandfather sleeps just through the fence on the other side
the same sun shines on them all
the same earth holds them
the same river still sings.

Planting Apple

It was cold, the day
we planted Apple.
The church flowed with locals.

Some didn't like the Filipino priest
or his lacy gown
'like a christening doll' -
a voice behind me hissed.

Some coughed
exclamation marks
Oh Really?
at certain parts
of the eulogy,
others coughed
at the censer-
swinging
ceremony

but we all listened hard
to the piper who played
at the head of the line
to show her the way

as the cold song of time
piped through the big pine
and her final sun set
in the cemetery.

Rabbits

a dirt road leads to Deeban, past
granite boulders bunched like giant marbles
on a plain of winter-killed thistles -
silver gelatine tones
luminous, interrupted
by stark weathered bones;
trees in a droughtscape, moon-ruled
beside a man-made lake

you've come to shoot rabbits
in a place some call sacred

a spotlight stab cues movement
all at once, in sync, all the ground
seethes and teems as sinuous flesh

the land dances!

drought dance, starvation
bone dance,
austere agony
trivialized by light and water

dying rabbits pour
in eddies and flows
so closely packed no soil shows -
live interactive Fibonacci swirls
a fur-clad dance of death

you can't shoot, look away
while others wade knee deep, hit
with rifle butts like cricket bats *thwack!*
as floods of rabbits surge and burst around them

you turn and watch the sterile lake
misinterpret moonlight
instead

Numeralla Dreaming

Snakebite

when the snake bit
low on his calf
he thought he'd been shot

and staggered

time froze, made clear
perfection of yellow tussocks
in strands of shadow
below the blue glass bowl
of sky. a flicker
something disappearing
like a cloud
or a thought

then panic, all time
at once, rushing
arms, legs, heart pump
while a calm inner voice
recited the litany

'don't panic
immobilize the limb
apply a pressure bandage
call for help'

leaping the fence
and falling, caught
entangled, winded
screaming 'no!
this is not where I will die
these ants, that magpie'
up again, running
for home,
haven

he burst through the door
to ordinary sunlight
on the floor, the tap
slowly dripping
desultory flies, legs up
on the window sill
carnival tinkle
of wind chimes

Numeralla Dreaming

from the orchard

too much at once
in his head —
the phone, but the ambulance
is hours away
the neighbour, but today
he's at the sales in town
the pressure bandage, but no point
by now the poison's
well distributed

puncture marks wide apart
a big snake; if brown
or tiger, maybe an hour
from the strike. how much
time does he have,
what is the end of a life?

starts a note
dear tom and belinda
but can't think of what to add
except
love, dad

decides to die in bed
lies down, head full of visions
sound of blood
pumping poison

recalls the mess of death
all the liquids draining
won't leave that mattress
for the kids

grabs the whisky
saved for a child's wedding

stumbles through the yard
to an old car up on blocks
sits in the back seat
drinking
waiting
to die

and wakes
next day
with a headache
when his neighbour arrives
with the kids,

Numeralla Dreaming

looking for him

empty bottle
the world returned –
yellow -
he's still not sure
if it's heaven
or hell
though

Snakescript

dusty quiver
in the middle
of the Big Badja bridge -
we both froze, tiger snake and I

did he see me as clearly?
head raised, his perfect
overlapping intricacy
of scales, belly pale
his alien eyes, dark flame
tongue flicker, feline
cold gold

then he poured forward, slipped
away like memory
his glyph
left scribbled
in the dust

Spring berries

before winter I gather
pine needles from under
the cemetery trees
to bed my strawberries

how sweet each spring
Ann Pettigrew
1861 – 1882

Numeralla Dreaming

Steve Primmer

his years are weights
he carries eighty

his scythe jerks
but the ears sigh down gently

he gathers a sheaf
for his sister's grave

she drowned here seventy years ago;
each spring he grows her wheat

Numeralla Dreaming

The day the camels came

It was unexpected, I have to say
coming down the Humpty Dumptys
on the way home from
a day in town
and there they were

padding past Bob McGuire's
mares paddock,
strung out in a line –
five camels

three big,
one with a man on
and two smaller, darker than the others
then I was up the other side, and gone.

Everyone saw a different number
even Euan, who pastured them that night
wasn't sure how many there were
or where they were going.
Some said the camel herder
had flowing Arab gowns
but for me he was
just a stockman.

Nothing really happened
except, in the way we keep track
of time round here,
things got linked
to the camels.

Talk of water tanks, the need
to fill them immediately
or watch them blow away
and someone will say
'Look at Jeff's tank!
Fluffy had to duck
when it blew down to the river
that time the camels came.'

Numeralla Dreaming

When carp first appeared
in the trout river,
when the fire brigade burned
the koala colony,
when our garbage dump
became a recycling depot;
all camel time now.

The Folk Festival when
the chick who gave good head
below the campfire by the river
turned out to be a bloke

the day the camels came to Numeralla.

Numeralla Dreaming

The fox

The track, uphill through shaley rock
meant I must bend, watch where
I set my feet. Heat
thrown down from cloudless sky
reflected from the ground
in waves of sound, cicada cacophony
spiced by eucalypt and the cloying
musk of dog bush.

A flash
like sensing the presence of a snake
fixed my eyes on the ridge above;

a fox
as still as I,
each strand of auburn pelt
distinct, separate -
in that frozen moment
I thought I knew
how Durer felt
etching his hare.

The only movements I saw
were a twitch of white tipped tail
straight out-stretched
and a wrinkle passing over
his nostrils'
black patent leather -
then, in a parabola
of wild perfection

he vanished.

Numeralla Dreaming

tickling fish

begin before the river
think slow, break pace
approach crouched, become
something always there, air
or tussock – move loose, windblown
onto bank, hand spread as twig, immerse
through surface - pause for cold shock
waver over stones, become ripple, feel
real kinship with water
wander fingers as weed drift
think tendrils in current
concentrate on trout
drowsed in safety
softly brush touch
under overhang
along walls, mind-form
form and shape from
momentary contact
hover until
swift instinct strike
(your hand
has always been
a weapon)
let it work
jerk once, feel
gill grip
flip up and over
quicksilver slime shock
solid pulse of life
alive, alien on grass
fast dying brightness
slit, offer back
gut and gill
fill your sack
with shabby treasure
river won't remember
but you will

Numeralla Dreaming

Author bio:

I was born in Kaitaia, attended school in Napier and left New Zealand to live in Australia in 1969, returning home only briefly over the next 40 years, spending the last 25 in Numeralla. In 2007, recovering from a broken leg, I started writing. In 2008 I returned to live in NZ, and completed a Diploma in Creative Writing at Whitireia Community College in 2009. I went on to graduate from Victoria University in 2011 with MA in Creative Writing.

This collection and grateful thanks addressed to Numeralla NSW where the writing began.

www.ingramcontent.com/pod-product-compliance
Lightning Source LLC
Chambersburg PA
CBHW070044070426
42449CB00012BA/3156